The Recovery Poet
Coffee & Cake

The Recovery Poet
Coffee & Cake

By Stuart Hardy-Taylor

Published by:
Little Nell Publishing at The Old Curiosity Bookshop
2019

Little Nell Publishing at The Old Curiosity Bookshop
2019

Copyright ©2019 by Stuart Hardy-Taylor

All rights reserved. This book or any portion thereof may not be reproduced
or used in any manner whatsoever without the express written permission of the
publisher except for the use of brief quotations in a book review or scholarly
journal.

First Printing: August 2019

ISBN 978-0-244-50921-7

Little Nell Publishing at The Old Curiosity Bookshop, 115 Loughborough
Road, Hathern, Leicestershire LE12 5HZ

www.oldcuriositybookshop.co.uk.com

A copy of this book has been deposited with the British Library according
to the Legal deposit Libraries Act 2003 and has been sent to: Legal Deposit
Office, The British Library, Boston Spa, Wetherby, West Yorkshire LS23 7BY.

Additional copies will be sent to Bodleian Libraries University of Oxford,
Cambridge University Library, the National Library of Scotland, the National
Library of Wales and the Library of Trinity College Dublin on their request.

Reach Out

Who should read this book?

Anyone with any kind of addiction problem, and all the Charities and Services who are there to help: The drug and alcohol teams, the police and prison officers, GP's, clinic and hospital A&E staff, paramedics and ambulance crews. I hope that this enables you to understand us a little more, to help more of us into recovery.

If any of the poems in this book have touched you, the reader, or if you can identify with any of these experiences:powerlessness, desperation, and helplessness, but turning into strengh and hope that these poems depict, and you have had enough and want to find that new way to live, free of addiction, then please reach out...

If you the reader, or one of your loved ones is suffering in their addiction, or through a loved ones addictions, then there is hope for you. I found that hope in God and the worldwide fellowships.

Helplines

ALCOHOLICS ANONYMOUS.
National Helpline: 0800 9177 650 OR
help@aamail.org

NARCOTICS ANONYMOUS
National Helpline: 0300 999 1212

COCAINE ANONYMOUS
National Helpline: 0800 689 4732

There are also helplines and fellowships for the families and friends of those who suffer addiction. We all cry, but none of us needs to suffer it alone. Contact these fellowships for support and advice:

AL-ANON.
National Friends and Family Helpline: 0800 0086 811

FAM-ANON
National Helpline: 0207 4984 680

Disclaimer:
The poems in this book have not been officially endorsed by any of the above charities and fellowships, neither do any of them have any affiliation with me, the book, or each other. They are there purely as an information source for those seeking help

Contents

Introduction

Hello,
My name is Stuart Hardy-Taylor, and just for today, I am a very grateful recovering addict.

I took my first mind- and mood-altering substances at the age of twelve along with cigarettes; and from this very young age, I found a way to change how I felt.

I grew up in the town of Loughborough in the UK and had a great childhood up until the age of twelve when I started to feel the need to fit in with the 'in-crowd'. At that time, the in crowd were the punks and skinheads of the early 80's and it was here that my addiction and my addict was born with my first addiction, which was to solvents and butane gas.

At the age of sixteen I found a new crowd when I started hanging out with my brother and a new set of mates and it is here I had my first pub pint and I can say today as I am in recovery, that from that first pint, my drinking was different. I was downing pints and wanting the next and this never really stopped for the next 27 years until I came into recovery.

At the age of 17 going on 18, I found a new set of mates again and this is where I met drugs through the start of the rave and dance era and my football years, I took to drugs like a duck to water.

Substances made me a promise from that first sniff of glue, they promised me that they would help me fit in with the crowd and help me be someone I thought I should be or help make me someone I didn't want to be.

Substances promised to help me escape from the things I suffered as a child, substances promised to comfort me in times of hurt and pain, they promised to help me forget life, they made me a promise and I put my trust in them all my life.

BUT THEY LIED AND THEY NEVER SHOWED ME THE COST, FOR ALL THEIR HELP TO ESCAPE AND THE TEMPORARY COMFORT THEY WOULD BRING.

Addiction had ruled my life and through the denial and the walls I put up, I lost everything and that was the cost and is the cost of addiction and what you have to pay for promises of what drink and drugs have to offer if you want to choose their way of life.

It cost me, my wife, my son, my home and job and almost my life, BUT MY ADDICTIONS ALSO COST THEM AND ALL MY LOVED ONES.

But my life looked normal to the outside world, but the truth is, that I drank and took drugs nearly every day of my life, my life was centered on getting drunk or high.

Until in my brokenness I cried out to God and then I went into treatment at THE CARPENTERS ARMS Rehabilitation Centre, where I started to learn that life without substances is truly possible with the help of a loving God and a recovery programme.

I admitted that I was powerless over my addictions and then I started to recover from my life un-manageability, and now today I live an abstinence-based lifestyle and I am handling life on life's terms.

This book of poems depicts and informs you of how I have come to this place in my life today. The title 'Coffee and cake' is how recovering addicts live their new life, meeting friends and support workers in café's and coffee bars, instead of our previous haunts of pubs and drug dens. The title represents our new life and I hope that anyone who reads this book, whether addict-addicted or addict-free or family and friends of the still suffering; gets the message and passes it on, because

TOGETHER WE DO RECOVERING

STUART HARDY-TAYLOR

THE RECOVERY POET

Acknowledgements

I would like to say a few Thank You's…

To my God and Saviour Jesus Christ. Thank You for never giving up on me and paying the price for my sin and freeing me from my addictions.

To my ex-wife and son. Thank You for still letting me be a part of your life, my sorry is in my recovery. To honour the promise, not today as a husband, but still today as a father and forever 'still family.'

To my family and friends who have stuck by me, I love you all.

To my Dad who got to see me free of my addictions. I love you always Bah Stu.

To Swanny, Rachel and Jackie, who helped me get into treatment and to all my soup kitchen family, you made me possible, Thank You.

To Bryan and Judith Spence and everyone at my beloved Carpenter's Arms. Thank You for breaking me and making me, my heart will always be in the 'Carp's' and with the lads.

To Rev. Peter Lolley, thank you, my heart received the truth and tough love at times, which was what I needed.

Through the love you showed me; you and Denny will always be in my heart.

To Mr David Innes and Mr David Cross, you both taught me so much and gave so much encouragement for writing my poems in the early days. If it wasn't for you both, then this book may never have happened.

To my Pastor, Paul Garner, and all my Church family at the Beacon Christian Fellowship. My love for you all flows from my heart, through the love you have all shown to me.

To my Sponsor, Steve, you know more about me than my own Mother. Thank You for all you have done, and I'll love you always.

A massive Thank You, to the fellowships and to every recovering addict and alcoholic, for giving me the message that we do recover a day at a time. The love I have for you all, is in the therapeutic value of one addict helping another.

For those addicts who are yet to find the rooms, or who have lost their way and wondered off, come on in – you are the most important person in the room. Recovery and love and freedom awaits you...

To Lynda-Lou Coyle, PA extraordinaire. Thank you for all you do for me and all those in and out of addiction.
Last, but by no means least, my confidante and best friend in recovery, Jerome. Thank You for teaching me how to stay humble and for showing me the ropes. The only words I can say are Thank You and 'loves ya man!'

WARNING

THIS BOOK CONTAINS SENSITIVE DEPICTIONS OF ADDICTED LIFE AND THROUGH THE VERY NATURE OF ADDICTION, SOME STRONG LANGUAGE HAS BEEN USED.

THIS IS NOT TO OFFEND, BUT AS THE AUTHOR AND THE PERSON THAT EXPERIENCED AND LIVED THE LIFE THAT MOST OF THE POEMS IN THIS BOOK DEPICTS, I FOUND IT HARD TO FIND OTHER WORDS TO EXPRESS HOW I FELT ,OR HOW THE LIFE OF ADDICTION REALLY IS.

HARDCORE ADDICTION

I want to talk about addiction, And the kind that stops ya breathing,
Yeah, I'm gonna tell ya about addiction,
And the kind that gets ya wife and kids to leaving.

Let me tell ya about addiction, the kind that makes you suicidal,
For addiction is a war zone that has ya fighting for survival,
And let me tell ya about addiction the kind that's taking parents from their kids,
For Yeah addiction is the killer, placing all our loved ones under lids.

And addiction is the taker that will never let ya win,
The Crack pipe, beer can, digging with a pin.
Crack house and homeless, in the alleyways their dealing,
Addiction is insanity that takes away ya feelings.

The One brown, two white, sniffing charley then ya hooked,
Men are dying from addiction and pretty girls are being robbed of all their looks.
Breakfast bowls used for ashtrays and mould is growing in the cups,
Whilst mommas in the bathroom throwing up her guts.

Daddies in his armchair, drinking, chuffing on the weed,
Babies crying for a nappy change hungry for its feed.
Neighbours call the social and send them to the door,

Because the house is just a pig sty and there's crap all on the floor.

The addicts come and go cause there's dollar to be made,
Police rock up with a door ram, shouting it's a raid.
And it doesn't stop them using even though the kids are gone,
Compulsion and obsession keep the using going on.

Parents always scoring, grafting robbing from the shops,
Town centre curfews, running hiding from the cops.
Now Mommas doing favours just to get her fix,
Whilst daddies in the big house serving on a six.

Rehabs and probation put on a DRO's,
Stops him on the brown but the beer and spirits flow.
Slump in the toilets with head in the urinals
Another addict dead, cause that last hit made it final.

Another addict bagged, means another brother in the chiller.
Recorded Accidental death, but ADDICTION was the killer,
The reaper counts the bodies, whilst the coffin maker counts his takings,
And all up and down the country family's hearts are breaking.

But another addict's death won't stop the drug abusing,
For Addiction and denial keep the suffering addict using.
Shaking in morning and sweating the beds,
Alkies running from their past and the voices in their heads.

Beer is their blood and the drugs are in their veins,
It doesn't matter what the poison the addict name is still the same.
Drop out and scum bag, dirty stinking thief,
Bag head, crack head, lying robbing cheat.

Started with a few lines, clubs and pubs and bars,
Now he's drunk and suicidal and sleeping in his car.
Wife and kids gone now, job and house stolen by the coke,
Yeah this is the true nature of addiction and it's no laughing joke.

Mums are looking ill whilst dads are emaciated,
Kids are bullied at their schools' tears running down their faces.
Clucking on new sentence, again rattling in a cell,
Heavens not a crack pipe and smack's a living hell.

Pin cushion body parts, neck and groin and feet,
Hostels, flat crash, sleeping on the streets.
Families make decisions on burials or cremations
Addiction is a killer that is sweeping through the nation.

Though it isn't just the addicts that suffer this affection,
Because everybody suffers, when faced with
HARD CORE ADDICTION

PRAY
GOD HELP US ALL
AMEN

ANOTHER'S PAIN

Mothers, Fathers, Sister, Brothers, Sons, Daughters,
Grandparents, Nephews, Nieces, Uncles, Aunts and friends,
have all lived our addictions. This poem is for them.

There's pain in every needle and there is pain in every empty
glass
There's pain in every broken promise; of this time is the last.
There's pain every snorted line and every pill that's popped,
There is pain in every mother's cries, why can't my baby
stop?

There's pain in every lie and from the parents, there's pain
with every stolen pound,
There is pain in the families' mourning, as the coffin is being
lowered in the ground.
There is pain within the children's eyes; when mummy and
daddy part their ways,
There is pain at the children's parties when either parent
don't turn up on the day.

Oh, and there is the pain we cause ourselves by every
selfish act,
But it don't compare to the pain we cause our loved ones,
when we just keep going back.
There is pain in every weeded paper; and every spliff that's
smoked,
There is pain in a father's heart, when the dream for his son
it has been broke.

There is pain within their worries knowing their child has nowhere to lay his head,
There is pain with a policeman at the door, delivering the message that every addicts parents dread.
Oh, there is such pain with telling their child, that they are no longer welcome at their door, there is such pain with the realization that they cannot do no more

There is the pain of the same old story they have heard time and time again,
We think we're the ones who are suffering, but we don't feel another's pain.

ADDICTED LIFE

This is a hard-hitting poem about life as an addict.

He's a Class A drug taker and he's feelings for shaker,
He's misery maker and she's family heart breaker,
From a mother's purse stealer to street kid dealer,
He's no pain feeler and he's quick fix healer.

She's a big-time drinker with a life's wasted sinker,
And he's lazy lout stinker and an only self-thinker,
He's an absent father with a heart getting tougher,
There's no food for his wife and his kids' lives are getting
rougher.

She's a no damn giver because he's a prison cell liver,
And He's shop door sleeper with a night-time shiver,
She's a street breast bearer and an easy sex sharer,
She's a loud street swearer and a no shame carer.

From a play yard prankster to a nightclub dancer,
Onto a night-time gangster where violence was the
answer,
He's a hardened user and past forgetter,
He's a morning shaker and a sweat bed-wetter.

Oi oi, she's ex hard-core raver but she still loves popping
E's,
And he's a rehab hopper, with tracks in arms and past D
V T's,
She's a recognized face and street time blagger,

And she is lost in the world of the ten bag shaggers.

He has no flesh on his bones and he's all sunken and thin,
And he's trying to find vain as he's digging with a pin,
He's on first name terms, with chemist where he goes to get
his meth's,
And they're all in and out prison for petty crimes and petty
thefts.

Chemical cider, crack, vodka and lager, speed and then
brown,
Weed, spice and Charley and prescription drugs being sold
about the town,
Addiction never sleeps and it never takes a rest,
Addicts are lying to support workers, when they're going for
their tests.

Death from overdoses, addicts stabbed up with a knife,
But this is just a normal day when you live the
ADDCIT LIFE.

IN THE QUIET TIMES

This is a poem from the heart of every addict. We are not having fun, addiction is not a laugh, we do cry, we do feel, we run, we escape, we fear, we are sorry, we want life. BUT WE DIE, IN THE QUIET TIMES.

In the quiet times I cry and in the alone times I weep,
It's In the quiet times I hurt, when I'm unable to sleep.
It's in the me times I'm in pain and they are the times you don't see.
When in the quiet I am haunted by all my past memories,
In the quiet times I'm reminded of all the secrets I keep,
The images my past always shows me of me abused in a heap.

In the alone times I am scared and I'm afraid just to think,
But I only let you see what you see, through all the drugs and the drink,
The silence it cuts and reminds me, just like a razor Sharpe knife,
Of the shame that's not mine and the guilt that has ruined my life.
But you look to me as being dirty, like some dirt on your shoe,
But I wish you could spend a moment in my madness and see the things I went through.

And so, take this is invitation for you to come and share in my past
Come live again the times, that I care not to remember and let's see how long you last.

I liked you understand me and know me and just acknowledge how I feel,
And just understand, that the drink and the drugs is just the way that I heal.
And today the way that I am, do you really think I'm happy and proud?
Because some days in the quiet times I can't rest because your judgement is too loud.

The condemnation I feel, at the end of day when I am alone in my head,
The resentments and hatred I feel, through all the junkie and piss head comments you've said,
The lack of self-worth is compounded by the voice in the night,
Making me not to awake in the morning, because I know again it's you and addiction I must fight.
But every day is the same and through the drugs and drink I'll just run, and I'll hide,
For I need to block out the things I remember and change the way I feel deep inside.
But I never woke up one morning and just decided to be an addict who sleeps on the streets,
And I do not enjoy getting the money I get by asking you to throw cash at my feet.

This is not the life that I chose and it's not what I really wanted to do,
But I bet you would be shocked and amazed, just to know that I used to be you.
Yes, I had love and a family, a job, a car and a home,
And that is why in the quiet times I weep, when I am lost and alone.

For I was charged and sentenced to life in addiction but innocent of crime,
But that's through the damaging secret I keep, as I cry in the quiet times.

JUST ONE

This poem carries the most fundamental message for any alcoholic, that it is the first drink that does all the damage.

I know if I listen and I take just one drink,
Then Its gonna lead to two,
And if I have that second drink,
Then two becomes a few.
So now I've had a few beers,
I'll push it just one more,
What started out as one drink,
Has quickly turned to four.

So now I've had the fourth drink,
The addict comes alive,
Now he's taking over,
And he wants to go for five,
He convinces me real easy,
As I down the fifth,
Saying Son, we're on a roll now,
Ya might as well have your sixth.

See now the addicts happy?
Because now we're up to seven,
And it's now he starts to mock me,
As seven becomes eleven,
But at this stage I'm starting,
To really hate myself,
For now, here comes self-pity,
As I'm going past the twelfth.

And so, this is now the danger zone,
And I'm tearing at the seams,
Because this is now no-man's land,
And I'm drinking in the teens,
But the addict starts to laugh,
Because he's proud of what he's done,
And now we start to argue,
Because once again he's won.

So now I'm at the anger point,
Who cares about the amount?
Because by now I've really lost it,
To pissed to keep a count,
But it's at this point we're both drunk,
And we both lay down in a heap,
But it's always on my own I wake up,
In the car park where I sleep.

And so once again I've woken up,
Guilt ridden with what I've done,
Why did I let him tempt me?
Because I know it starts with one!.

DON'T LISTEN TO THE LIE,
ONE IS NOT OK!

LAST BREATH

Addiction wants everything and it will take it. I think that's enough said, I'll let the poem speak...

I looked at my addict and I asked him just why,
Did you have to break all the pieces and leave me with tears in my eyes?
I looked up at my addict because I was down on one knee,
Begging and pleading please let me go free.

I have nothing left and I've no more to give,
Have you not took enough, please just let me live?
My marriage you took, my wife and my boy,
You took all my happiness and a heart filled with joy.

Self-respect and self-worth, my appearance and health,
You broke me that much that I couldn't sit with myself,
You gave me a heart, that was cold like a stone,
A heart full of self where my pity made home.

A life running on empty and my tank had run dry,
And the world was like the hard shoulder, with life passing me by,
I looked at my addict with my arms open wide,
And said you took all I've got, there's nothing inside.

I screamed at my addict, I have nothing left,
My addict looked back and said
"THEN I'LL TAKE YOUR LAST BREATH"

HUMAN ADDICT

This poem is for those who don't know anything about drug addiction. Please read it and try and understand me.

You call me a scumbag and you call me a thief,
But you do not see all the pain that I'm in and this man underneath,
And you call me an addict and you call me a drunk,
But you do not see the dark depths of my life, to which I have sunk.

Before I had a life and a family and by them all am I missed,
Do you think I like this life of addiction, everyday being drugged up and pissed?
I don't want to be robbing your houses and stealing from you,
In fact, I hate myself in addiction and all the things that I do.

And I'm tired of fighting and scamming and doing time in the nick,
It's no fun having the shakes in the mornings and seeing all the blood in my sick,
I don't want to be injecting myself, drinking and shoving drugs up my nose,
Do you think I like sleeping rough on the streets and wearing dirty torn clothes?

Can you not see the state that I'm in and my state of appearance in health?

I hate this disease of addiction and slowly I'm dying, can't you see that I am killing myself?
See I was young when I started; I was scared, I was just a young kid,
I was bullied and abused as a child and a life in addiction is where I have hid.

The alcohol it numbed the pain and the drugs took the hurt straight away,
But then soon addiction grabbed me and then I needed them every day,
My whole life's been a struggle, I've never known who I should be,
I've spent my whole in a prison, but the prison was in me.

I am not looking for pity, because I know sometimes life is not fair,
I am only asking you to see me as human and maybe then you will care,
I spent my life in addiction and to authorities; I'm just a number, a name on a file,
And I'd love to laugh like you all do and would love to be happy and able to smile.

Everyday inside I am crying, because I am so scared, but I've had to harden my shell,
You have fight for your worth, when your life's in addiction and you're living in hell,
But today I am not talking just about me, but how each and every addict has felt,
But to take away the drink and drugs from an addict, we need support and your help.

So, take all the substances away and then see what you have left,

A recovering addict with passion and saving others from death,
So please before you pass your judgement and hand me my shame,
Please look past my life in addiction and ask me my name.

And If God can forgive and break me free from my chains,
Then who are you to condemn me and refuse to help me to change,
If God can forgive and transform and help me be free,
Then why can you not see past my afflictions and really see me?

THE PARTY'S OVER

Hard-core raver, drink and drugs,
Eighties, nighties football thug.
Gift of the gab, virginity stealer,
Face about town, party time dealer.

Designer clothes with wide boy swagger,
Pub tarts, nickers off, full time blagger.
Pill popping, acid dropping, young weed smoker,
Piss taking, street fighting, cheeky lad joker.

Sofa surfer, floor sleeper, tit nip sucker,
Bouncer taunting, fearless, cocky little fxxker.
Dance tents, dance clubs, white cloth gloves,
Micro dots, purple oms, loved up doves.

Smart dressed, face straight at beginning of night,
No pull, no sex, start a fxxking fight,
Mouthy, ralphies, timberland, lacost,
Pissed-up, drugged-up could not give a toss.

Stand up merchant, girl heart breaker,
Whizz dick, can't cum, orgasm faker.
Big fish, little fish, cardboard box,
Cocaine, base dab, whizz upon the rock.

Get up, work hard every single day,
Graft hard, party hard that's how I used to play.
Eighties, nighties this is how my life was run,
Laughing, joking when it was just for fun.

Chilling, come down the morning's aftermath,
These are all my memories from when it was a laugh.
Young kid, carefree, wild boy rover,
Lights out, book closed, because I got addicted, So for me the party's over!

BROKEN PROMISES

I feel this poem needs no explanation

Shut and banged and violently slammed, once again
there goes the door,
The door that separates us, because once again I've
broke my promise;
I have broken it once more.

The last talk of separation, the last fret of us splitting up,
Was quickly soon forgot about and so
once again, our marriage was in a rut.

I would try and toe the line, by drinking less, at least it
seemed so to her face,
But my alcoholic life was lived upon the edge,
In fear she'd find the empty cans all hidden about the
place.

She would always do the talking and I wouldn't hear the
things she said,
Never did I have the balls or the right to argue back,
I would always just tell her, to fuck off inside my head.

Drinking and drugging in secret and I thought I was never
quite that bad,
But twenty years together, she could always tell
The amount of drink or substance that I'd had.

Why did I always hide it and why did I always have to
push it and then have to tell her lies?

Because most of time, there was no way I could have hid
it,
As the truth was right there in my eyes.

The days when I would stumble, when I found it hard to
walk,
Yet another argument I'd caused, because,
I would always slur my words when I tried to talk.

In the morning she'd confront me, and she wouldn't
shout or get irate,
But she would make me feel guilty and tell me I had to
stop,
before she didn't care and then for us it would be too
late.

But I just couldn't stop the drinking, no matter what she
did or what she said,
I drank my marriage down the drain and through my
addiction to the alcohol,
My marriage it was dead.

We both had our problems towards the end, with money
debts, drink and the weed,
But she was the bravest one of us both, because she
was the one to make the decision, to take our son and
leave.

I still believe that she had love for me,
but she wanted our son free of the drugs and all the
drink,
And I think deep down she knew the place that I was
heading,
she knew my sanity was on the brink.

Today, I now accept my part within the marriage breakdown,
and I accept her walking out with our son right through the door,
Because I know that if I'd made another promise,
I'd have broken it, just like all the other promises that I'd broken before.

IT IS ALL OF THESE

A Truthful depiction of what addiction really is.

Dirty, horrible, stinky and smelly,
Consuming fire inside your belly,
Violent and twisted and vile thought provoking,
Strangulating hands around your neck its choking.

Lives and hearts all around are breaking,
Ability to love and feel from you it's taking,
Smoking, joking, laughing, lying and crying,
Escapism, prisons, hospitals, coffins, dying.

Compulsive behaviour crazed and wild,
Maternal feelings stolen from the wanting child,
Futures, past and present become heavy loads,
It weaves a tangled web and makes us walk such
crooked roads.

Robbing and cheating, fighting and stealing,
Selling sex, beatings, MacDonald's toilets and alleyway
dealings,
And hands held out with begging mouths, can ya spare
change please,
The devil, the illness, isolations, the mind diseased.

The pub, the club, the wedding, the party, celebrating
birth,
Even when committing a fellow addict back unto the
earth,
Taunted lives, minds attacked, mocked and teased,
This is addiction and it is all of these.

TRUTH HURTS

Fast walk, sunken cheeks,
Baggy sports clothes, slurry speech.
Need a fix, roll a fag,
No teeth, ten-pound bag.

Hoodie up, baseball cap,
Scammed someone, got a slap.
Not much to eat, micro meal,
Giro cashed, spent on deal.

Dirty clothes, no laces in shoes,
Need haircut, dosh spent on booze,
Sports direct, Adidas, Puma, Nike,
Dealing drugs, stolen bike.

Owed dealer cash, got black eyes,
Mate od'd, shit he died.
Just out of prison, we were friends since three,
He'd packed it in, he scored for me.

Why can't it stop, vodka, red bull?
Too wacked, too pissed, missed the funeral.
Mates death makes me think,
*Addicts life, it f*ing stinks.*

I'm getting help, I'm gonna stop,
Don't want to die and be forgot.
I'm pulling up, don't want the shame,
I'm moving on, deal me out the game.

COCAINE

The party starts and ends when charley turns up,
because at some point the disco lights get turned off and
it's no fun dancing on your own...

It's cunning, it's cold, and it's calculating, it's confusion within
your brain,
It is callous, it's cruel and captivating, it will make you go
insane.
It's creative, its carnivore, and it's copulating, it will make do
things, you do not want to do,
Its crude, its crime, its cash and it will take every last penny
from off of you.

It's commanding, its courage, its camaraderie, when in the
toil its you're sharing a line,
Its comeuppance, it's captured and its court case and now
you're on your own, in prison and serving your time.

Its calamity, its camouflage, its cantankerous, it will not let
you have your say,
Its capture, its capitulate, it's captivity, if hooked, it shall rule
your mind and life every day.
It's carefree, it's casual, it's a catalyst and things change,
But in reality, they stay the same.

It's cartels, its contracts and currencies. Purifiers, pushers
and dealers, take the money, but shun from taking the
blame,

Its catchy, it's catching, its celebrate, it's at weddings,
funerals, parties and births
Its chaos, its charisma, it's a charade, it robs people from all
they're worth.

Its civility, its claustrophobia, its cocky, it robs your family,
It steals food that our families should eat,
Its collusion, its colossal, its comatose, your dead within your
eyes,
But still, your walking about on your feet.

Its comfort, its comedy, its common, its available,
its attraction is openly shared,
Its compelling, complacent, compulsive, feelings you have
For your loved ones, are challenged attacked and impaired.

Concealment, conceit and confusion,
Shall rule the way you live and the way that you think,
Consecutive, consistent and conspicuous,
Will be the things you lose and the depths to which you shall
sink.

Its continuous, its contemptuous and its contemporary, its
fashion,
Its film, its pop, and it's art,
Its controlling, convicting and corrosive,
It will steal your soul and it will blacken your heart.

Its cupidity, its culture, its culminate,
what goes up must always come down,
Its curt, it's a curse, it's a circle
And if you do not break the circle, you'll just keep going
round.

Its complications, complicated and non complis-mentis

And your mind is never your own,
Its concussion, its condolence and condescending
And it will take away family your friends and your home.

Its confidence, it's confident, it's confidential,
You'll only believe in the power of you,
Its conflict, confiscation and confinement,
It will place restrictions on all that you do.

Its constraint, its constraining and consternation, anxieties
and depression and fear, will touch every part of your life,
It's cornered, it's a conundrum and it's care-less,
Your life is balanced on the edge of a knife.

Its contamination, it's contagious and contentious,
You'll rob and steal off the people you love,
Its contemptuous, its contradictory and its contrite,
You'll receive no peace, unless you look up to God in the
heavens above.

It's convenient, its convert and its convincing
And you shall hang on to all the lies that you're told,
Its convivial, its convulsions, its cosmopolitan,
Its worldwide, purified, smuggled and sold.

It's corrupt and its costly, it's covert, it's isolation from the
world,
'Cause in the end you'll run, and you'll hide.
Its craving, it's credit, it's a creditor, your wealth and your
health shall dip
And your appearance shall vastly subside.

Its crestfallen, its criminal and its crooked,
You're unable to look at family and friends in the eye,
Its culture, it's cumulative and it's culpable,

On the outside you laugh, but inside you cry without knowing reasons to why.

Its custody, a custodian and a curmudgeon,
Tempers and moods shall be tested and frail,
Its cyclical, it's cynical, and a custom,
Detrimental devastation it leaves in its wake and its trail.

Its cryptic, it's cunning and curious, I pray you never start and from its power you must always refrain,
Its crucifixion, it's crying and it's your coffin
And it's the killer that's known as
COCAINE

ADDICTION WANTS IT ALL

This poem says it all in the title and I need not say any more. The message in the words will explain everything.

Cocaine sniffed and beer drunk like water,
Took away my family and my bricks and mortar.
The pills and acid that I've popped in my gob,
Took away my licence and my driving job.

Ripped up fags, Rizla packed with weed,
Helped build my illness, my mental disease.
The drink and drugs that I've sunk, and I've drank,
Helped drain all the money that I had in my bank.

'Cause addiction takes and it never gives ya back,
And never needed help from the smack nor the crack,
I never smoked the white and I've never pinned the brown,
Though never did it stop me from sleeping on the ground.

For I lost what I lost, and I lost at a cost,
But addiction made me numb so I didn't give a toss.
Oh, the pain and the hurt and the tears that I cried,
I laughed on my face, but I'd died inside.

And I was tired of being sick, and sick of being tired,
But every day I still woke up, pissed and wired.
For its hard and its rough and its cruel and it's tough,

And one's too many and a thousand not enough.

I was young in life and I didn't have a clue,
And it all started off with a little sniff of glue.
And the fags and crime, mixed butane of gas,
Led to me taking drugs and drinking beer on mass.

I was an armchair drinker while chuffing on the weed,
But the more stuff I took, the more stuff that I'd need.
Yes, addiction it robs and wants to take ya life,
And never will it stop with just ya kids and ya wife.

Addiction it lifts and then it lets ya fall,
And never can you satisfy addiction,
Because addiction wants it all.

MIRROR'S TRUTH

Yes, that IS you in the mirror...

Take a long hard look in the mirror,
Will you still deny and ask for further proof?
For you know that denial is getting harder,
Because you know that the mirror tells the truth.

The image that you see and still deny,
Is hardly a recognizable image of yourself,
But still you carry on causing damage,
to your family and your heath.

The mirror does not lie; the mirror gives a reflection,
 A reflection that's real and true,
So how long do you think that you can carry on denying;
That the man in the mirror is actually really you?

You've got to look for self-acceptance,
Admit what you know and to what you see,
If you keep on denying the mirrors truth;
Then I'm sorry, forever addicted shall you be..

THE INSANITY OF IT ALL

This is how my life was before I went into the Carpenters Arms Rehabilitation Centre. I was never homeless, but through the insanity of my addiction and the isolation my addiction drove me to, I would walk the streets alone, drunk, and I would often sleep in town centre car parks. I had dens in the woods around town and I would also sit on the streets and in the shadows and alley ways within my pity and brokenness.
   BUT NOT TODAY, PRAISE GOD AND THANK YOU, RECOVERY AND THE CARPENTERS ARMS FOR BREAKING ME FREE!

Through the night I'd walk and not a moment have I slept,
For I'm drunkenly stumbling about and unsure about my steps,
And I'm haunted by memories of things I have and haven't done,
Whilst I'm searching my memory, to find where my troubles began.

The insanity of my behaviour "WHY?" Cold and dishevelled the streets I'd roam,
And sleeping in car parks and woodlands whilst I had love, a bed and a home.
And I'd hide from the streetlights, at times, for the want of not being seen,
Not wanting to show my appearance, of addiction, unwashed and unclean.

46

In the 24-hour supermarket, in the toilet mirror, I cannot bear to look at myself,
But just after throwing my guts up still another beer I remove from the shelf.
The hours seem to drag, and the drunkenness hasn't the power to speed up time,
What have I done to deserve this torture? and where was my crime?

See I'd wander around in the shadows and Inside I was crippled by rage,
And I wanted to find a way out, but drink and drugs had the key to my cage.
I'd watch the other drinkers, homeless and addicts, congregate outside Mackie D's,
Asking everyone that passed by can ya spare any change for me please?

Ya see I was holding on ever so tightly but it's hard not to slip further, when your life's a slippery slope,
But I could see my rock bottom approaching but I had no fight left, for addiction had robbed all of my hope.
But I knew the place I was heading because when I closed my eyes, the picture's I'd see,
Of my family and son at a funeral, It was mine, they were burying me.

But still the images didn't stop me, and my selfish life was the drink and the streets,
I just carried on roaming and drinking and still stumbling about on my feet.
I didn't want to mix with people, nor did I want to be with my family at home,

For I was killing myself slowly and if I'd die, I'd die on my own.

This point was my lowest, suicidal thoughts coming at me thick and so fast,
I wondered if I would see tomorrow, or did I really care if today was my last?
I'm not writing these accounts just to shock, these events, feelings and emotions, are not a lie,
Because whilst at the bottom of the pit of addiction, you don't really care if you live or die.

But that was the stark reality, for I knew I was killing myself,
But for another drink, on my belly I would have crawled,
That is my life in addiction and that's the insanity of it all.

Thank you.

STUART HARDY-TAYLOR

48

AFFLICTED MAN

Total abstinence is the key to my recovery, the thinking that I am OK with just the one, is the same thinking that lost me my family and home and also nearly my life. It's the same thinking that got me into rehab and kept me in addiction for 32 years. RECOVERY QUOTE: "one's too many and a thousand's not enough"

I cannot afford to take a sip or even touch a drop,
For I am an afflicted man and do not know if or when I would stop,
Because when I drink there is a compulsion, a reaction within my brain,
That makes my thinking crazy and then my behaviour becomes insane.

And then my loved ones suffer because I become so self-obsessed,
Then life becomes a struggle and then I end up in a mess,
And If I were to drink again, my life would again be on the slide,
For a drink or two would not be enough for the man that lives inside.

I am living with the affliction of addiction, which means I'm always on my guard,
Today I have to work a program and some days it is quite easy, but some days it's bloody hard,
Some days I have fits of jealousy that I can't relax like others and have a drink,

But other people can put the plug back in the hole and not wash their lives right down the sink,

But that's the affliction I suffer, some people cannot eat peanuts and some need food that's gluten free,
But I suffer with the affliction of addiction, which means I can never again put a substance inside of me.
So every day I check my behaviours, feelings and emotions and I do not look for perfection, I just do the best I can,
Today I live a life that's in recovery, but never do I forget the power of addiction and that I'm an afflicted man.

DENIAL

This poem is how our addict will lie to us and mess with our heads and say we haven't got a problem

You haven't got a problem; there is nothing that you need to overcome,
The problem is in your head my friend and you are safe with just the one.
I'm not saying that you have to drink a load and I'm not saying go out upon the piss,
But you have been sober for a while now and a little can, wouldn't harm or go a miss.

I wouldn't want it like it was before, drinking the whole night through,
You haven't got to buy a pack of eight my friend, just maybe one or two.
Don't worry about tomorrow, after tonight you will be able to stop again,
This time it will be different, this time it won't be the same.

You cannot live your life this way because you'll never laugh or smile,
And if you think that sobriety will bring you happiness, then my friend, I'm afraid that it's you who's in denial.

THE REALITY IS:
The reality of my problem, is repeated throughout my history,
My history tells honestly, that I cannot put a drink inside of me.

Denial can make me stumble but then reality pulls me back,
History shows me memories, of the power that I lacked.

Never could I buy the one or two and make them last a night,
The compulsion for more alcohol, in me would cause a
massive fight.
To think that I could have that one, is today what makes me
laugh and smile,
For today I live within my sobriety and not the illness of
addiction caused by your denial!

DIS-EASE THE DISEASE

Throughout my life I have felt at Dis-ease with myself and so when I came into recovery and heard this term "THE DISEASE OF DIS-EASE" it all made sense

Depression and addiction, had me an anxious wreck,
I was haunted by my past; I was scared about my future,
which looked so dark and so perplexed.
From a young age addiction had always plagued me,
But I did not see when depression came to play.
Depression had crept right up on me
and I found myself living in unknown fear, each and
every day.

It started out as a whisper, the voice inside my head,
which would mock me, laugh and tease,
I kept this hidden from my family; outside I was always
smiling,
But inside I was crippled by dis-ease.
Then I could not carry on any longer, everywhere I went,
People were saying, that Stuart's a happy bloke.

But my wife had begun to notice and when she asked me
about my moods,
I snapped and then I broke.
She forced me to the doctors, telling me I was sick and
ill,
The doctor listened while I was crying and then he sent
home,
With a little box of pills.

The pills did not really help me;
They did not change my thoughts or the way I used to think,
Because they did not stand a chance, to help me with my depression, Because I was addicted to the drink.

Home and work was getting harder, the sides were getting slippery,
Within my darkened hole
Depression ruled my mind set, while addiction and anxiety,
Had imprisoned my heart and soul.
And then there came that day, when she said that she can't do it,
That day I lost my son and wife, the only colours that I had left,
In this, my darkened blackened life.

Now depression and addiction, would often confine me to bed,
I could not stop the voices, so I would just try and shut them up instead.
Daily alcohol and drugs, would for now help me win the fight,
I'd dance and play in daylight, but then alone,
I'd cry and scream out through the night.

Every night; I'd punish myself into a stupor, whilst listing,
To heart breaking saddened songs,
And the voices where getting louder, telling me of ways to end it
And finally, rid of my wrongs.

I lost my home and job and by now I was drinking by the hour,

I lost my worth and lost my pride and for weeks on end,
I did not wash or take a shower.

Suicide, it ruled my thoughts, I could not focus on my life
and I lived in the hell of what I'd done,
Addiction and depression, was now beginning to affect,
The parental feelings, which I had towards my son.

My thinking was so selfish, I just constantly thought
about my problems
And I thought myself
My depression was getting deeper, whilst my addictions
were getting worse,
And causing damage to my health.

See depression has a stigma; I never wanted my friends
to see me slip,
Because some people don't understand and some think
they're being helpful,
Telling a depressive to get a grip.

Depression and anxiety; mixed in with drugs and alcohol,
Took me to walking in the darkness, insanely drunk
throughout the night.
I would sleep car parks and bushes, hiding from society,
Keeping my appearance out of sight.

But I always summoned the courage, to go into the shop
o buy more beer,
The excessive compulsion for alcohol, would always
overcome,
my anxieties and social fears.

Then one night I'd had enough, I was dying, and I went
down to my knees,

I cried out; GOD I know I'm killing myself and JESUS I cannot stop me drinking, CHRIST, won't you help me please?

This is where my life changed, God, he started to work within me,
And he was giving me strength to cope
And through the weeks that followed, as I listened to his word,
My life began to change, and my heart was filled with hope.

As I went into rehab, I felt that Jesus Christ was by my side,
It was here I spoke I about my past,
I did not run to the bottle and I did not run and hide.

In rehab Jesus spoke to me and God also told me of my worth,
So, I gave my life to Jesus and I prayed that God would take my pass away.
So I could live anew, in what would be my second birth.

I was baptized and cleansed with water, for my life in Christ Jesus to begin
I knew that soon as I emerged from out the water, that Jesus Christ my saviour, had removed me from my sin.
Rarely now do I suffer, from the crippling conditions,
That took me too my knees
God has taken away my fears and healed me of depression
And healed me of dis-ease.

Disease or as in another term dis-ease, is a common term which is used
In the circles of recovery, I am no expert, but when I first heard this term I understood it totally.

Having felt at dis-ease with myself for many years, maybe since childhood,
I now THINK that the onslaught of depression, anxiety and addiction
Was inevitable for me, but I now know that in Jesus Christ,
I can overcome anything in this world.

AMEN

THE BOTTOM OF THE GLASS

There is no answer in the bottom of the glass,
The answer that you seek will not be there,
The reasons will not be found,
And neither shall you care.

For when we are a drinking, we have no care in mind,
We forget out problems and then leave them all behind.
We loved to laugh, and we loved to joke,
But that was long before we were bounded by the yoke.

The yoke binding us that clouded the way that we think,
All the years wasted while in denial of the drink,
A five percent beer, thirteen percent wine or even a forty
percent shot,
Will not sort or ease the problems that we have got.

Learn to laugh at ourselves and not to impress,
Ending up the clown in a drunken mess.
We hate to look into mirrors and see what we see,
Because the reflection looking back is not who we should
be.

The drinking has to stop, and this time it has to last.
Sort out our problems, place them in our past,
And realise the solutions are not
In the bottom of the glass!

ADDICT STATISTIC LIST

*We are only lying to ourselves and just playing the
waiting game and this poem says it all...*

Who you trying to blag son, c'mon who you trying to kid?
Don't be another addict statistic, laying under a wooden lid,
And if you're lying to a mentor, or if you're lying to your peer,
You'll forever be imprisoned, crippled by addiction and
attacked by dread and fear.

Because you know you're only lying to yourself, but inside
you know the truth,
But still you keep on lying and searching for further proof,
You have to stop the lying, accept you have a problem, to
release you from addictions jail,
Don't become another addict statistic, waiting for the
inevitable and that final driven nail.

You have to embrace recovery, get help to stop the circle, of
getting high or getting pissed,
Take your name from off the grave and don't let your name
be added
To the addict statistic list.

EVERYWHERE HOME

With backpacks and their sleeping bags, around the cities
and towns they roam,
Living in doorways or hidden tents and that's because
everywhere could be their home.
Churchyards and soup kitchens, are so often the places they
can be found,
And everywhere it is their home, but their beds are always on
the ground.

With Fresh air every morning and there is always the promise
of an open view,
But never is there any hot water, central heating, or windows
to look through.
No toilets, mirrors, showers, no sofas and no tables, nor
sitting upon a chair,
No washers, no cookers, fridges, no bedroom with a bed, at
the top of the stairs.

For everywhere it is their home, and anyone can see where
they all live,
But not everyone in the comfort of their own home, with a
thought to them ever do they give.
For everywhere is their home but they have no cupboards to
be bare,
And with no walls or doors to stop the people; who would
want to look and stare.

And their door it never has a number, but they may have a
disused sign above their heads,

As they try and sleep with the fear of being homeless, as we sleep safe and sound within our beds.

So, spare a thought as you just walk by talking on your mobile telephone,
You have just walked through someone's lounge, kitchen, bathroom and bedroom,
Because that person sleeping on the street, everywhere is their home
I always say to the lads in the treatment centre, when addiction books a holiday, let me know and I'll have a day off recovery. It's never gonna happen...

ADDICTION NEVER SLEEPS

Addiction waits for no man, addiction will always put you to the test,
Addiction never takes a holiday, addiction never takes a rest,
Addiction is always plotting deceitful lying schemes,
Addiction's always working hard behind the recovery scenes.

Addiction is always training pumping iron in the gym,
Addiction is always waiting, for that opportune moment to slip in,
Addictions in the classroom learning about the latest recovery tools,
And addictions not selective, for addiction will always suffer fools.

Addictions watching body language and how the recovering addict speaks,
Addiction is sat with us in the doctors when we are feeling ill and weak,
Addiction is in the invitations, to weddings or a party at someone's home,
And Addiction loves to get us doubting in all the times when were alone.

Addiction's always working, drawing maps, working on new paths or a different way to find,
For addiction is looking for that open window or that unlocked door which leads into our minds,
Addiction's in the smiles of friends that we haven't seen for years,

And Addiction tries to stop us going to meetings and sharing with our peers.

Addiction will sneak in when were happy and it's always with us when we are sad,
Addiction will trick us into thinking that we're worthless, sick and mad,
Addiction is always with us and I'm afraid it's in our lives for keeps,
By all means take a rest in your recovery, but never take a day off because
ADDICTION NEVER SLEEPS

ADDICTION'S RUT

Addiction is just like Groundhog Day, nothing changes, if nothing changes...

Leaning up against a wall, I'm purely leaning because I can't
stand tall,
Stumbling about and it's hard to walk, I'm slurring words
because I'm too drunk to talk,
A broken drunk sitting in town on a bench, coughing and
sputtering with a sickly stench,
Dirty clothes, unclean am I because of drink, unwashed and
unkempt I start to stink.

I find it hard, for myself to fend; I pray, how many more years
till my torments end,
Once a husband, a father, a family man, but now a drunk,
immersed in drink and empty cans,
Top designer clothes, for weeks on end I've worn,
Laced with hot rock burns, along drunken falls, which made
holes in knees and elbows torn,
Bearded face and lager breath along with fag-stained teeth,
A car park bed, with a cardboard quilt and a frozen me lay
underneath.

A liquid diet, no solid food within my rotting gut,
But every day was the same, when I lived my life in the
Groundhog Day of
ADDICTIONS RUT.

ADDICTION DON'T FIGHT FAIR

It's anything to win against ya addict

Go on, knock him out, knock him out; hit him left and right,
Punch him, kick him, nut him, addiction don't fight fair, so go
on, smash him, gouge and bite,
Knee him, drop him; lay him out, then stamp the fuckers
head,
Baseball bat or metal bar use anything to win, because that
bastard wants you dead.

Crack him, twat him, elbow, bottle, gun or mace,
Addiction has no Queensbury rules and whilst my addict lay
there dying, I'd spit in the wankers face,
So, for me to fight my addict, I'll use any method, or any
weapon and fight any way I can,
Because my addict will try any method, to hurt and kill this
man.

So, when you fight addiction, just remember that for you,
addiction doesn't care,
Just remember that addiction fights real nasty and that when
ya fighting addiction,
Addiction don't fight fair.

ADDICT'S DREAM

If you want to gain sobriety or if you want to be totally clean,
Then both can be a reality, it hasn't got to be a dream.

But if you're lost and still dreaming, I can promise, that
dreams do come true.
Only you have to be willing to accept you're powerless, if you
put any substances inside of you.

A young boy when my nightmare started, 32 years of
addiction I have fought,
But 6 months I spent in rehab and now I practice methods of
recovery that I was taught.

Now the lesson that I duly learnt and the way it works and
how recovery should be practiced and forever done,
Is if you're strong enough in your own recovery, then help a
fellow addict to dream the reality and escape addictions
nightmare and walk in freedom in the Sun.

I HAVE A NAME

Addict, Crack head, Skag head, Alchy, Piss head. It is what we are but it's not truly who we are.

I have skin and I have bones,
I had a wife, a child and a home,
I have human blood running through my veins,
But I have damning memories that would cause me pain.

I have fingers and I have toes,
But I have secrets that no one knows,
And I have a nose and I have ears,
But I learnt that Drink and Drugs take away my fears.

Like you I breathe in air because I have lungs,
But I've run away from my past life since I was young,
I can see you all because I have eyes,
But you don't see me, because I'm isolated, with my true self internalized.

I have a brain that's inside my head,
But it was all the above that took away my family home and bed,
I have hands and I have feet,
But now I live and sleep upon this dirty street.

I have arms and I have legs,
But you just see the homeless addict that sits and begs,
I still have hair and some of my teeth,
And I am still a human being underneath.

Yes, compared to yours, my life a mess,
But I am still a person that's made of flesh,
Yes, I can be anyone that you know and love,
Anytime, one of your loved ones, could suffer all of the
above.

Yes, I'm made up from all the things that you are too,
So as I sit here on the street and in the doors,
Just remember I'm still flesh and blood and one of yours,
But you probably haven't been through the things that
I've been through, and although our lives may not be the
same,
Please remember I am a human being and yes, I still
have a name.

DRY

This is one of the first poems I wrote in Rehab, with Addict Soldier. Not sure which came first, but it was these poems that started my journey.

Coats and Hoods, and Brolly's, are the things that keep us all dry,
But dry for me now has a different term,
Because for me dryness is something I have had to learn.

Once I was soaking wet although not with the pouring rain.
I was drenched in alcohol and I was crippled by its pain.
At time's I drank so much, immersed in over my head,
Swimming and drowning in addictions pool, of beer I would have to tread.

Then one day I was tired and could not swim no more,
I was sinking fast and so I had to turn and find the nearest shore.
Here is where I found myself at the Carpenters Arms front door.

Now no longer does addiction, make me scream and cry,
And no more do I need to ask the why.
That's because I no longer drink, for now today,
I am two months
Dry

CAFÉ NERO RECOVERY

I wrote this poem whilst sitting in Café Nero, early one morning, just after coming out of treatment. Nero's was a big part of my early recovery and is now my unofficial office! Thank you, Nero's, I am eternally grateful.

Look at me, first thing in the morning sat drinking lattes in café Nero,
Only just six months ago, that drink would have been a lager, percentage 5.0.
In the morning I'm feeling better, for not drinking through the night,
My eyes are bright, my head is clear which inspires this poem I write.

I couldn't have written this poem while drinking way back then,
My hand would have been too shaky, to grasp or hold a pen.
But now my hand is steady, rock solid, as I hold this coffee mug,
And only ever looking backwards, too full in the hole I've dug.

**So, my life is so much better, so much better by a mile,
I've replaced the corner shop, for café Nero, latte and a smile!**

STORY OF A DRUNKEN MAN

*Acceptance is a massive part of recovery and this is a
poem full of the acceptance of my addictive behaviours.*

All the abuse that I put me through,
And what started out as just one or two,
The lying, stealing, deceitful cheating,
Drink and drugs and under-eating.

Convicted guilty and in un-repentance,
And addictive denial was my life sentence,
Secret drinking, life always sliding,
Secret using, buying, hiding.

Tortured thinking, drinking throughout my life,
Has now driven away my son and wife,
And through the unopened bills upon the floor,
Through addictive behaviours of always wanting more.

Days spent in bed as I procrastinate,
And days off work and always late,
The depressive truth of how far I've sank,
With the realization of no cash in bank.

House repossessed and now forever the door is locked,
And yet another thing that I have lost,
Lost and broken and back again with mum and dad,
And alone with the painful memories of what I once had.

And so back in the room where it all began,
But mine is yet just another saddened story
of a drunken man.

ADDICTION'S SCHOOL

We need a change in recovery policies. To understand us, try asking us...

Too many wanting bodies and not enough recovery beds,
Far too many alkies' and addicts are getting off their heads,
Too much pain is written on too many broken faces,
Too much money wrongly spent, in purely money-making places.

Too many fresh-faced students that know how to talk the talk,
They've read it in a book, but have they ever walked the walk? Too many people and politicians telling us how the war on addiction should be won, Too many people and politicians, that have never seen needle or a crack pipe and don't even care how our war begun

Too many ignorant people, don't know the death rate within the addict masses,
And the rich and well-to-do's that don't think that it's their problem,
As their money keeps their addictions hidden within their higher classes,
Addiction affects the rich man and the poor man, it will always cause a rot,
Hundreds, thousands and even millions, addiction costs us money and it wants every penny that we've got.

The best way to fight addiction is to directly face the problem, get suffers clean and get the drunks from off the streets,

Let's get them into rehabs, let's give them hope and build them up, let's give them an education to pull others to their feet,
Because pull addicts from their prisons of addiction and find the one's that aren't a fool,
Find the ones who can make a difference, find the ones who've been educated with qualifications, from life's
ADDICTIONS RECOVERY SCHOOL

ENCOURAGEMENT

IF ANY OF THESE POEMS ENCOURAGE ANY ONE PERSON INTO RECOVERY THEN THEY HAVE ACHIEVED THEIR PURPOSE

I do not proclaim to have all the answers; I cannot see life's hand of cards,
Neither can I predict the future; but I know it's gonna be really hard.
I can only wake each morning and take it day by day,
And I'll tackle all life's problems whenever they come my way.

I know I can never take it easy; I know recovery is not a joke,
For me, I cannot afford to be complacent, not even a fag to smoke.
And if I see an old mate, I may have to walk the other way,
Because to find me in a relapse, I'd be like a needle in the hay.

Therefore, the way I'm going to do it, I'm going to pass on all I've learnt,
I'm going to show other people in addiction all the clean days that I've earned.
Please this is not a lesson for I have no power to preach to you,
But have faith that you can do it and that faith shall guide you through.

Recovery is all about the patience, do not rush what is to come,
Remember where you are today and be proud of all you've done.
I don't have all the answers; but if you do, please tell me,
for I myself would like a clue.

I only write these poems as encouragement, for myself,
And a hope they may give encouragement to anyone of you.

THE FIRST STEP, TELL US YOUR NAME

Reaching out is the first step to freedom, but also the hardest one. But in the fellowship's rooms you are not alone, and you will be understood, even in your silence.

It starts in the rooms by saying your name,
But we don't care what's your poison, and ask were lays the blame,
Because in recovery, it's about exposing the root,
To realise our triggers, that makes us, drink, shoot, or toot.

See it could be a person, a moment, a loss, that sets off the alarm,
Our emotions and our fears, that make us self-harm,
But we don't burn, we don't cut, we don't need sleeves to hide what we do,
Our scars are inside, kept well out of view.

See people don't realise that addiction is a master in stealth,
Stealing our lives and playing roulette with our health,
Addiction will rob us, and it will take all we have left,
It will keep us on playing, until we draw our last breath.

So, to beat our addictions we've got to do all that we can,
Truth is, addiction don't care when the shit hits the fan.
So, to get ourselves free and stop drugs and be clean,
We need solid foundations, good people, a network, a team.

I thought I was clever, I played the game on my own,
I lost my family, lost my job, my pride and my home.
So please don't be proud, for the ice you walk on is thin,
Don't go it alone, because alone you won't win.

So, take the first step, there's no need to feel shame,
Just get into the circle and tell us your name...

FROM ONE ADDICT TO ANOTHER

When I was in Rehab, there was a saying "LIVING THE DREAM" Well today I don't live the dream, because every day I dreamed of not drinking or taking drugs. "TODAY I LIVE THE REALITY" RECOVERY IS TRULY POSSIBLE TOGETHER WE DO RECOVERY

I that pray all addicts hear this open invitation,
I pray all addicts hear this heart felt plea,
Come live life free of drugs and alcohol,
Recovery is truly possible and from addiction you can be free.

For I too was ravaged by addiction,
Every day in addictive pain I'd scream and shout,
But then I started to listen to other addicts in recovery,
Who began to show me a new way out.

Being an addict isn't easy; but being an addict in recovery,
You'll never be on your own,
For living as a recovering addict;
There'll always be someone you could talk to; someone you can phone.

In recovery we are a family; were in this all together,
As a sister to a brother
I promise you that recovery is a reality
And that's FROM ONE ADDICT TO ANOTHER

SUPER ADDICT

Now then, I love this poem, this is a little bit of fun but with a serious message. We think we are invincible and like superheroes when using drugs, but the truth is, we are not. Our super powers made us powerless

Clarke Kent, he used a phone box but me I used a line,
Because when I snorted cocaine, I thought that I could fly.
Iron man was ordinary until he wore his suit,
And that's the way that I was, until I had a toot.

Yes, I was super addict thinking no one could drink and drug as much as me,
And after I took that first one, using drink and drugs was my super-power ability.
The famous Wolverine, was super powerful with his massive claws,
But put me on the Charley and I'd be invincible and knock out f*ing Thor.

Dr Jekyll would turn into, the nasty Mr Hyde when he drank his potion,
And if lager was made of sea water, Aqua-Man would be homeless because I'd drink away his ocean.
He-Man would call on Grey skull when he took on Skeletor,
But I thought that I, was master of the universe when I kept on taking more.
When Dr Banner became all angry, he'd morph into the hulk,
But even he wouldn't stand an f*ing chance, if I couldn't have a drink and I was in a sulk.

Now the Flash, he was super-fast and could run at lighting speed,
But there's no way he would have beat me on a pick-up run, scoring me Charley and me weed.
In my head no one could ever beat me, when I was super pissed,
And although I'd feel in the morning, on the night that I was drinking, I'd take a right hand from Iron-Fist.

Now Batman had his enemies, like the Riddler, who said, "now riddle me this,"
And that must have been the life for my wife, because I was always riddling, because I was always super pissed.
And then there was the Penguin and the constant laughing Joker,
Like him, I'd laugh until I wet myself, because of me being a super-power smoker.

And if my wife was wonder woman, she wouldn't stop with her whip,
Because my super addict power was getting lager past my lips.
Yes, I was a super addict and always wanting more and more,
But Dr Doom was always waiting, and no super-hero could ever save me, not even The Fantastic Four.

Because I was a law unto myself just like the judge, they call Dredd,
But the only thing was, I was an enemy to myself, cause I was always getting off my head.
My super-powers helped me fit in with the banter from my Gob,
But when my super-powers ran out, I was just a drunken

mess, looking like swamp thing and the blob.

I wasn't like any other super-hero because my super-powers couldn't save,
The only thing that Addict super-powers do, is dig a faster grave.
So now I've taken my mask off and hung up my super addicts cape,
Because I have no need for my super Addict powers because I don't drink or even smoke a vape.

If you're a super Addict and you drink and drug the same as me,
Then be a real super-hero and hang up mask and cape for your loved ones,
And be who you're really supposed to be.

POWDER

This poem is a difficult one because I have had to depart myself from some people I would at one time, have called friends. But in recovery the realization reveals a revelation which is in the truthful words of this poem

When every day ya sniffing powder, your mind begins to
stray,
You forget about the important things and how to live, just
day to day,
See nothing really matters but getting that powder up ya
nose,
And every week you get a paycheck, but see how fast it
goes.

It comes into the left hand but goes straight out through the
right,
But that's the price you have to pay, for sniffing Charlie every
night,
And you really can't afford it, it's an addiction you have to
kick,
But then you think he's ya best mate when your dealer gives
you tick.

It's like living a life with plastic, when on tick the drugs you
lay,
Whilst dreading that certain moment, when your dealer tells
you to pay,
You know you cannot pay him, but you really want some
more,
So, you go and start another tab at another dealers door.

Now you've problems scoring, because you owe money everywhere,
And then you go and promise your dealer payment, but he really doesn't care,
He says he wants his money and he says he wants it fast,
Then you promise ya self that this time is gonna be your last.

But you now have the money to pay him, from the receipt of some PPI,
So, you go to pay your bill in full, but he sees that weakness in your eye,
Then before you know it, in his left palm you've placed six grand,
Then once again without thinking, you're taking a gram in the other hand.

So now your dealers happy, cause once again he's reached his goal,
And that's getting you back buying, keeping you hooked on his payroll,
And so many thousands of pounds I've wasted, on addiction that had me blind,
For all I wanted to see before me was a big fat powder line.

But I carried on wasting money cause I was a fool and couldn't see,
That the dealer weren't my mate and what a prick he made of me,
And by now I've bet you've guessed it that this stories mine and yes, it's true,
Listen, no dealer can be your best mate cause he just wants money outta you.

See the dealer will keep you playing, if you've money to play his game,
But he has no real care for you, he just wants to sell you his cocaine,
But now I've stopped the snorting, as my life was balanced upon the edge,
And this time I make no promise because this time I make a pledge.

So, listen Mr Dealer, you never were my mate,
You can keep on calling and even knock my door a little louder,
But no more shall I waste my life on you, and your dirty stinking
POWDER

FOOLISH FATHER

*ONE OF THE HARDEST THINGS I HAD TO
OVERCOME WAS THE PAIN I CAUSED MY SON. MY
SORRY IS SAID WITH ALL MY HEART*

Tears shed by foolish father,
Can make many ripples upon life's water,
I've shed many tears in life's waters pool,
Wrong decisions taken, which made this fool.

I lost sight of what my heart holds dear,
I can wipe my tears, but still my sons cries I hear,
I should have stood up tall and strong,
Instead I withered down, singing pity's song.

But never did the love I lack,
For it's the love of my son that has brought me back,
For now, I'm not the father I was before,
And a foolish father
 I shall be no more.

ADDICT BE ME

The best way for me to stay clean is to spread the message of Recovery that was freely given to me. I was once like you, now you can be like me.

Injected, smoked and snorted,
Feelings and faces become distorted,
Dabbed, inhaled and excessively drunk,
Cheekbones protruding and faces are sunk.

Drugs and drink and behaviour disgracing,
Emaciated addicts are searching and constantly chasing,
Stealing and cheating to families they're lying,
Russian roulette and by needles they're dying.

Street begging and robbing just searching for coin,
OD'd in a flat after shoving a pin in his groin,
Isolated by drink and all alone in his home,
The lone alcoholic is dying unable to pick up the phone.

Street girls they are beaten, called junkies and whores,
But they'll be out again the next night earning money to score,
Blankets and bags and street dirt under his nails,
And kiddies are crying because their mummies and daddies are locked away in jails.

Weed being openly sold and now so openly smoked,
Ya cannot walk down the street any-more without being constantly choked,

Foreign beer getting stronger and the drugs are getting cheaper,
Which makes work harder for coffin makers but easier for the reaper.

Families are mourning at funerals and they're filled up with rage,
Because our loved ones are dying at such a young age,
Yes, this poems hard hitting, but this poem is truth,
And addiction is killing more and more daily and cemeteries are full of the proof.

But I'm a recovering addict myself, saved by recovery and saved God's grace,
I don't see a thieving cheating lying scumbag, under that sunken scared face,
I see a person who's frightened and scared and who so longs to be free,
And that is why I will never stop working my recovery, in a hope that one day,
for that addict to be me.

ADDICT SOLDIER

I wrote this poem in Rehab and probably one of my first ones and a big shout out to David Cross for his encouragement. Thank you, you taught me a lot and helped save my life.

Are you an addict soldier fighting the battle of clean or smashed?
Are you the Recovery officer giving orders to stay off the lash?
Whichever your role in the battle, Time is going to be tough,
Especially when other soldiers have fallen as they didn't fight hard enough.

You can't help a fellow soldier if in the battle you're wounded yourself,
See this is your own war and you need your mental fitness and your fighting health,
But if you've won your battle and you hear a fellow soldier in pain,
You can now help them up and show them how to fight once again.

But being addict soldiers we're not fighting for country or queen,
Yes, we are addict soldiers and we fight to stay sober and clean.

IT WAS I, THAT MADE MY SON CRY

Every night when in rehab, I spoke to my son on the phone and heard his many tears, and every one of them was of my doing. But every tear I caught in my heart which I turned into a promise. I never want to see my son cry again because of my selfishness.

How can we shelter our kids, from the life we've led our self?
How can we tell them lies, while trying to hide the deterioration in our health?
How do we keep the secret and hide what we do and all we've done?
How do we think we're normal and this is ok behaviour to raise a daughter or a son?

See; from when they're tiny babies, we all say that they don't know,
But they'll find out for sure, as they age, mature and grow,
We'll try and tell our children that drink and drugs are not the way,
But my child has every right to comment, Dad, I saw you do them every day.

Yes, I've made mistakes, six months spent in rehab, I did my sentence and served my time,
But every day I felt his pain, because my son was also punished, for my actions and my crimes,
All the times I wanted to walk out and hug him, when on the phone he cried such painful tears,
I hated myself and my addictions; I hated my weaknesses and my fears.

But I had to focus on my future and tell myself this is where I've got to be,
I had to be selfish, but not selfish in addiction, but selfish in my own recovery,
For if I got up and walked and I did not stick it out,
And returned back to the life I had before, as the drugged up alcoholic lout.

Then how could I ever preach, that an addictive life is not the way,
There's only one way that I can do it and that's to be clean and sober every day,
I've now got to be a role model and show that drink and drugs, are not the way it's done,
I got to teach that once in the trap of addiction, it's so hard to overcome.

My poems maybe hard hitting and at times might just touch a nerve,
But yes, we have to be accountable and bear the guilt, of the pain that our children really don't deserve,
And yes, for me the truth it really hurts, for in my heart I have the pain, of knowing it was I,
I was the one that caused him pain; I was the one,
That made my little son
    CRY.

ESCAPE

The feelings and thoughts of escaping through our feelings and emotions, can come from nowhere and can be dangerous to those in recovery. This is where we need to practice our programme and make it a 'we' programme and pick up the phone. Just like 'Who Wants To Be A Millionaire.' If your head asks a question and you don't have the answer – Phone a friend!

Sometimes I get those uneasy feelings around running and escaping,
When my emotions and life's mundane trails are growing and escalating,
And although in my daily life there is nothing really wrong, wanting to escape the way I feel can still be there and at times it can be strong.

And these are the feelings that sometimes come and just wash over me like a wave,
The dangerous thoughts and feelings that could send me to my grave,
For it is when fear and doubt come along and start to dance around with sweet temptation,
And they start to sing the euphoric songs, from my memory's past and about the sweetest of sensations.

And they try and lure me back with visions of how they used to make me feel,
Whilst whispering their lies of escape and of how it was only them who can truly heal,

And my mind it is so cruel to me, the way it comes to mock
and the testing times it loves to gloat,
Showing me carefree drug euphoria and the sensation of
how they used to make me float.

Helping me scape, outside of my emotions and my true and
inner feelings,
The world would be locked away, as I escaped my head and
danced around upon the ceilings,
But I must shut the thoughts and feelings out before it gets
too late,
And before I start to fantasize the thoughts and start to
insanely validate,
And this is where I must be alert, in shape and on my toes,
Because the thought of me escaping, can be rapid in the
speed in which it grows.

For I can't afford to let it grow and rapidly run its course,
I must attack it at the point of thinking and at its centre and its
source,
And I can never let it get me by myself and isolated and all
alone,
For soon as temptation comes, I shall pray and then I'm
dialing numbers on my phone.

For I must remember all I've learnt and all that I've been
taught,
And the number one rule of recovery is never stay alone
within my thoughts.
So now with the fellowship of my friends to be with me in my
thinking,
And I can stop the thoughts of escaping and the danger of
me drinking.

Because they help me to acknowledge and see the reasons why,
And they also help me clear my mind and to safely rationalise,
So today, I say I'm sober and I'm grateful and that the horse is still behind the gate,
Because today with my friends, I faced my feelings, fears and emotions
And together we beat the feelings to escape.

A HEARTFELT PLEA FOR MR GASCOIGNE

I wrote this poem just after coming out of rehab and hearing that Paul Gascoigne had just relapsed again. The response I saw on a Facebook page made me cry, because of the ignorance of one comment among the many others, that were heartbreaking. Wishing even more pain on Paul and because all because he suffers from is simply Alcoholism. Alcoholism is a killer and we don't need judgement; we just need help...

I write these words for Mr. Gascoigne and it's a special heartfelt plea,
Dear Mr. Gascoigne, I myself am an alcoholic, but today I am a sober man and today of alcohol I am free.
Thirty-two years I spent in addiction, all of my life a troubled man,
But today I have faith in God my Saviour and I have faith in my Saviour's plan.

I was broken and I was dying, when I went down to my knees,
I cried out in pain, "God save me because I'm helpless, I'm dying, Christ won't you help please?"
God led me to a Rehab, where I prayed, to gain the power that I lacked,
I prayed to God on a daily basis, I prayed and read the Word and he took all the burdens from my back.

When I came out of rehab, I embraced recovery built on the rock of God's foundation and not this world's grains of shifting sands,

I have joined in with recovery meetings, I have joined in with recovery fellowships and no longer, am I a one-man-band.
I'll reach out to every suffering addict, along with all my recovery friends,
Because I've learned that if we stick together, together, we can bring our torments to their end.

Mr. Gascoigne, for years I've watched you suffer, when I was down, and in the madness too,
And I hope that you don't mind, but I felt compelled to write these words to you.
Because of your fame and status, we all see you suffering within your fight,
And to be really honest; I don't think that we really have that the right.

I know nothing about you Mr. Gascoigne, but I have seen your battles, on the front pages of the daily news,
But believe me that I shall pray for you and ask God, to free you from the booze.
Whenever I got wasted on drink or drugs, the whole world never needed to know,
But you haven't got that anonymity, because the cameras are always on you and your suffering is placed on show.

I'm not saying I have the answers, I can only tell you about my story, I can only tell you what I know is true,
I placed my faith and trust in God and within the fellowships, both of them help me through.
So I write this poetic letter to you Mr. Gascoigne, and I hope you get to read this heartfelt plea,
Because I truly believe that you have the power to beat the alcohol, and as a sober man, you can live forever free.

NEW PAINTED ROOMS

This poem is inspired by the song "DARK BLACK"
by Kristina Train. After my wife and son left due to my
addictions, I would listen to the saddest songs I could
find and I would then listen to them over and over again
within a depressive self-pity state and I now call these
my self-harming songs, because every time I listened to
them, I would cry as they cut me deep.

All the walls were painted black and grey,
As I lived my life in the past of my yesterday's,
The rooms within my mind were all painted black,
And the paint upon my futures door, looked old and
cracked.

I lived in the memories, of the mistakes that I had made,
My brightness gone, grey was my life, the colours fade,
No more did I see, yellows, blues or striking reds,
Pity had painted the rooms, a lifeless colour inside my
head.

Addictions dullness had caused my life to break,
The paint on window frames of my soul, were now all but
flaked,
I'd lost a colour that always made me shine so bright,
My colour of love had gone and so my life became black
as night.

But still within my life, I had a colour that was pure and
white,

A colour that is always in my heart and shining bright,
And over all the matt dull colours, did this bright colour run,
For through all the black and grey, I could see the colours, of my child, my son.

Through God and him today, the rooms of my life are painted bright in a new-life green,
And my futures door is painted new, and open wide, to the brightest colours I've ever seen,
All the colours of the rainbow, Red, yellow, pink, green, orange, purple and blue,
Today all my rooms are painted bright, for through the darkened black and grey, the colours of my son kept on shining through.

I'M NOT PLAYING

This poem tells of the times I went out with my son and always my addict had to come, never leaving my thoughts and letting me be present in the Father and Son times. BUT NOT TODAY ADDICTION, NOT TODAY

Addiction, you can keep on calling,
You can call, three or four times a day,
I don't care how loudly you're knocking,
I'm not coming out to play.

You can bang the bloody door down,
And constantly ring the bell,
But I'm not coming out to play with you,
Where's the fun in playing in hell?

We used to have a laugh,
And together we had that spark,
But did you really have to be there,
On the days, my son was playing in the park.

And again, on the days I took my son out,
Playing football on the field,
You would always turn up,
And to you I had to yield.

And every time we hung out,
Drink and drugs, you made me take,
You made me a different person,
A failure and a fake.

So, go on, piss off, go away now,
Our friendship's at its end,
And I hope you're always lonely,
You don't deserve, to have a friend.

So hey, shout through the letterbox,
I won't listen to what you say,
For I am not your friend now,
And I'm not coming out to play.

WASTE OF TIME

We need to look at the way we treat drug crime, and once again, I feel the poem hits home on the issues around: "The revolving door of addiction in this country, created by the system and not just the using addict." (Quote attributed to Mr Kevin Dooley.)

Another addict sentenced, for petty crime and petty theft,
Banged up again in the prison system, where they have no spaces left.
Sentenced for shop thieving and other petty crimes,
Two more months spent in prison system with only one thing on their minds.

An addict locked away will not sort or eradicate the cause,
Once again, they'll be addicts stealing, unrehabilitated, when released back through the doors.
Addiction will not disappear by placing the sufferer in a prison cell,
We need to take the drink and drugs away and help release them from their hell.

Take the drugs and drink away, it doesn't mean the addict is dry and home and free,
I am a recovering addict and the drink and drugs where a solution, to the problem inside of me.

It's time to look at the problem properly and not just keep burying it underground,
Let's start to rehabilitate the problem, instead of sending the problem down.

Forty grand keeps an addict in prison, for the total of a year,
Compared with thirty-three pounds, to tackle the problem
directly, once they're removed from the drink and gear.

Locking the addict behind the four walls and banging them
behind the bars,
Without proper rehabilitation, they will again be robbing all ya
houses and stealing from your cars.

And I am not defending all of our behaviours and our actions
because yes, I know they're wrong,
But we need to treat a suffering addict as a patient, for a
progressive illness that is so strong.

They used to lock alcoholics and addicts in asylums and
throw away the keys,
Does that not prove that addiction is an illness? and often a
fatal mental disease?

This poem maybe hard hitting but upon your minds and heart
strings I want to pull,
The truth is, no matter how many prisons we build in the
future, addicts in addiction will always keep them full.

So, wherever there is addiction, there will always be death
and pain and crime,
Let's start to rehabilitate the addict and stop banging them in
a prison cell,
as it's just a waste of time.

IT'S A MARATHON NOT A SPRINT

Recovery is a daily race. The Bible tells you to train every day. 1 Corinthians 9:24-27 and 2 Timothy 2:5 Please read and attach it to your recovery and your life.

When in the race of recovery, it's about the winning and not just the taking part,
When in the race for sobriety, you have to want to win with all your heart,
To daily beat your addiction, you must push on with all your might,
And be like the Olympic athlete, training hard both day and night.

A runner will speak of self-control and the need for discipline,
And that should be the addicts aim before the race begins,
Set your sights upon your prize and believe in what you're told,
Don't think of bronze or silver, you have to go for gold.

So be like all the winners and see in their eyes they have a glint,
But remember when in the race of recovery,
It is a marathon not a sprint!

Never give up!

SOBER MORNING

This is a true poem of gratitude and I wrote this short prayer-poem just after coming out of rehab with not much money in my pockets, but I was so rich in my heart. Do a little volunteering give a little back and let the gratitude build you up, don't chase what got you into rehab, this is what I was taught

Yet another sober morning and I wake without the taste of beer,
Because yesterday I wasn't a drunk but a giving volunteer,
And although my muscles ache and it feels like my bones are breaking,
I'm happy to have this feeling, more than the retching and morning withdrawal shaking.

So, sound now do I sleep, not fearing another addictive dawning,
And again, I give my thanks to God, for yet another sober morning.

NO GOOD - JUST BYE

This is a Dear John letter to my addict, and it's called, "No Good - Just Bye." Because there was not and could never be, any good in my relationship with my addict. So just... "Bye."

This is one of the hardest things that I've ever had to do,
And that is come to accept, that I can no longer live with you.
See; you've beaten me down and you took control,
You've broken my heart and you blackened my soul.
We've been together for years and years,
But I've had enough now 'please' no more tears.

Too many times we've tried to change,
And; around and around in circles and we're back here again.
Yes; I can remember the laughs and all the things that we've done,
But in truth, these latter years, it wasn't a laugh and you weren't much fun.
I cannot believe that at times I chose you over the important things,
Believing in your lies and the peace you said it would bring.

Even when I was broken and laid out on the floor,
I turned too you and begged and yes you always gave me more.
When I was down, you were always real nice,
But in reality, it was you who gave me my problems and this killer vice.

Years ago, we started out as a harmless fling,
But you wanted my all and yes, I gave you almost everything.
I know together we have no future, for a while I need to be alone,
Yes, I'm sorting my life out, but this time on my own.

It's going to be hard to forget you, you're everywhere that I look,
On television, in magazines, papers, sides of delivery trucks
In everyday life, you'll be what I see,
In the supermarket, the corner shop, it's almost like your following me.
See now this really hurts, because of our split I'll have to lose some good friends,
But that's the price that I'll pay, because there's a means to this end.

But yes, it's true; you've taken me places I never would have seen,
But you've also taken me to places I never should have been.
I had love, but you hardened my heart, you didn't know what it meant,
See; your idea of love is vile, it's twisted, it's bent.

I wish I'd have woken up sooner and seen you for what you really are,
I could have saved all this pain; I should never have let us get this far.
I'm not sorry, I can't cry tears for you anymore; you don't care how I feel,
I can still hear you calling me, I won't answer you, do one, this is my time to heal.

Without you I know I have a future, I know I can live,

106

I want nothing from you, in fact you've got nothing to give.
I'm gonna walk away from you and yes, I'm gonna do it with some pride,
You haven't got a hold on me anymore, why should I be ashamed? why should I have to hide?

This time I'm gonna fix me, no more papering over the cracks,
Without you I can move forward, never needing to look back.
You're not worth my breath, you don't even deserve a goodbye,
I nearly took my own life and you were the whole reason to why.
You had the power to make look and feel happy, when in reality inside I was sad,
And you made me finance it all with every last penny that I had.

Oh, these last years were so painful and dark,
why did you have to push me so far?
From all the fun-loving days, just having a laugh with the lads, in the clubs and the bars.
We can't ever be together; I can never again be your friend,
Because you are my poison and your poison means my end.

You'll find someone else; I know that you will,
Sweet talking again, with drink, powder and pill.
So, don't ever come calling, looking for the reason to why,
Just please understand, that it could never be good

So, this is just … BYE.

THANK YOU

AND MAY GOD BLESS YOU ALL
IN YOUR RECOVERY

THE RECOVERY POET

STUART HARDY-TAYLOR